I0470390

GERMANY TRIP 1931 PHOTOGRAPH COLLECTION

This book is a collection of over 40 photographs taken in the August of 1931 in Germany and Belgium.

This is the first time many of the photographs have been put into print.

A list of some of the subjects the group of photographs cover are as follows:

ROYAL PARK BRUSSELS
ARCADE DU CINQUANTENAIRE
THE TOMB OF THE UNKNOWN SOLDIER - BRUSSELS
ROYAL PALACE OF BRUSSELS
HOHENZOLLERN BRIDGE - COLOGNE
COLOGNE CATHEDRAL
BRIDGE OVER THE RHINE - COLOGNE
4 OF THE 7 MOUNTAINS ON THE EAST BANK OF THE RHINE
RIVER RHINE FROM BONN
COLOGNE FROM THE RHINE
MARKSBURG CASTLE
BOATS OF THE RHINE
THE CASTLED CRAG OF DRACHENFELS
STOLZENFELS CASTLE
KOBLENZ FROM THE RHINE

THE ELECTORAL PALACE IN KOBLENZ
EHRENBREITSTEIN FORTRESS
PASSENGERS ON RIDE BESIDE RHINE
MUNICIPAL FESTIVAL HALL - KOBLENZ
STATUE IN FRONT OF THE MUNICIPAL
FESTIVAL HALL - KOBLENZ
PEOPLE ON THE RHINE
HOTEL ADLER - HINTERZARTEN
A BLACK FOREST FARM HOUSE
A BASKET SUNBATHING CHAIR
COW CART
OLD WOMEN IN THEIR SUNDAY DRESSES
ARRIVING AT CHURCH IN A BUS
LAKE TITISEE
PEOPLE RESTING AT LAKE TITISEE
HISTORICAL MERCHANTS' HALL FREIBURG
FREIBURG MINSTER
THE BLACK FOREST - HIRSCHSPRUNG
ROWING ON THE RHINE
BATHING ON THE BANKS OF THE RHINE
LUNCH ON THE BANKS OF THE RHINE
VIEW FROM RITTERSTURZ
BASILICA OF ST. CASTOR

Please note these photographs were taken Pre-WW2 so some of the locations might now look drastically different.

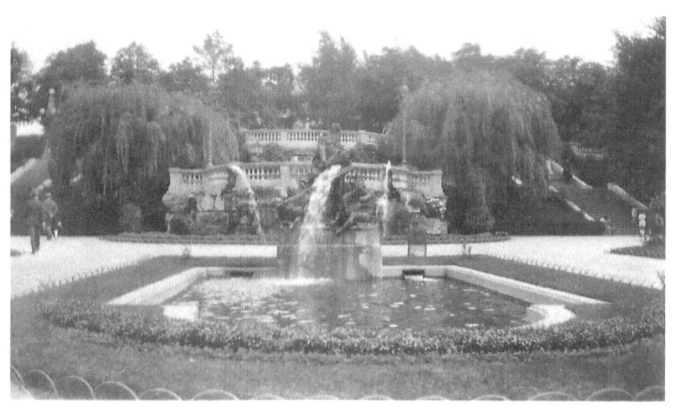

ROYAL PARK
BRUSSELS

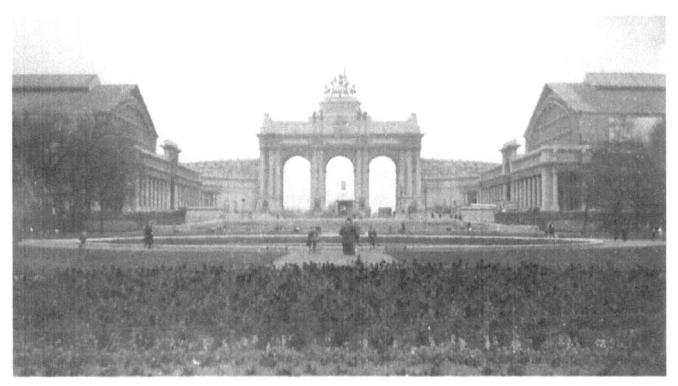

ARCADE DU CINQUANTENAIRE

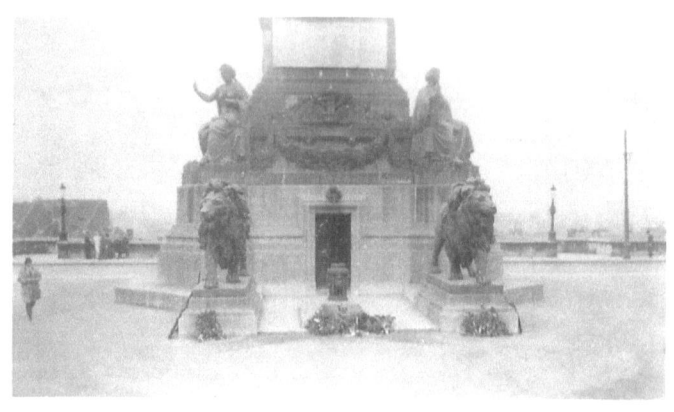

THE TOMB OF THE UNKNOWN SOLDIER - BRUSSELS

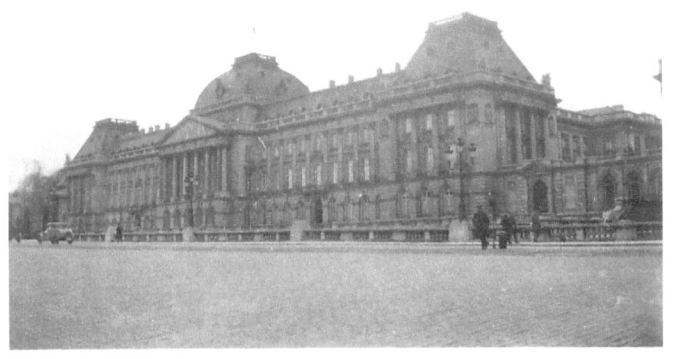

ROYAL PALACE OF BRUSSELS

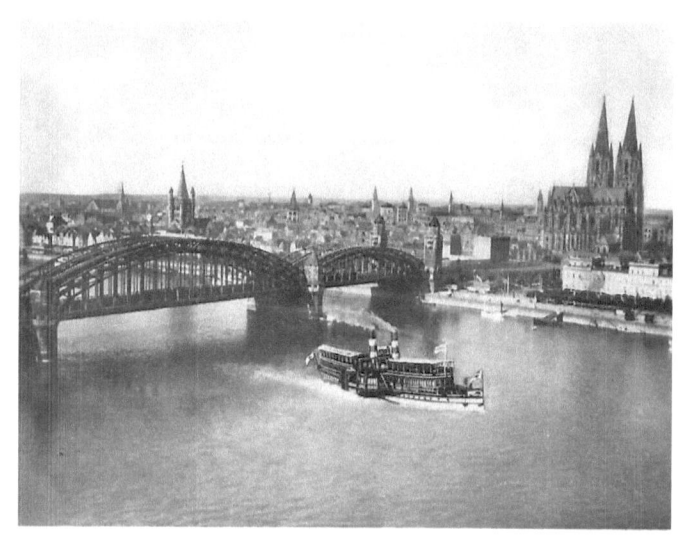

HOHENZOLLERN
BRIDGE - COLOGNE

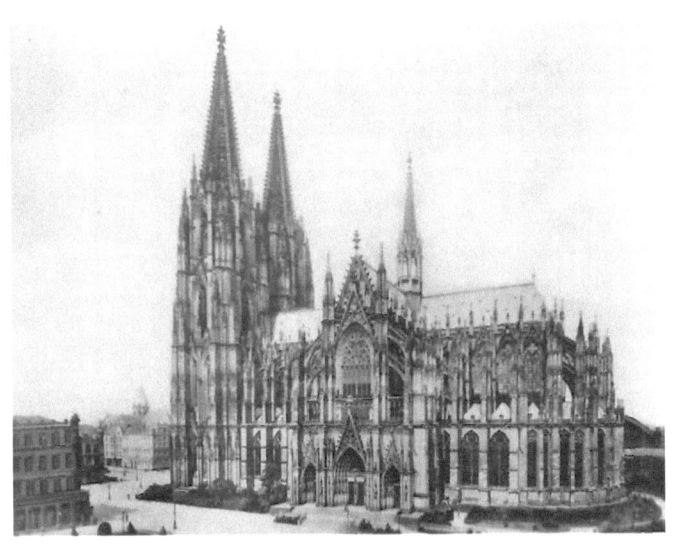

COLOGNE CATHEDRAL - SOUTH SIDE

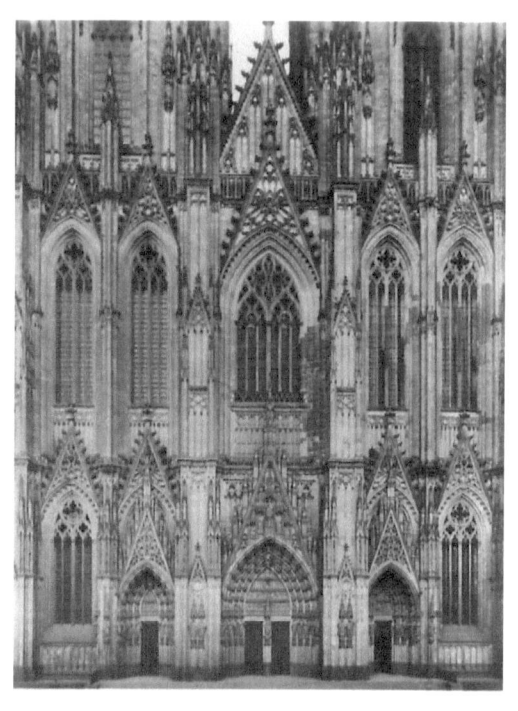

COLOGNE
CATHEDRAL - WEST
SIDE

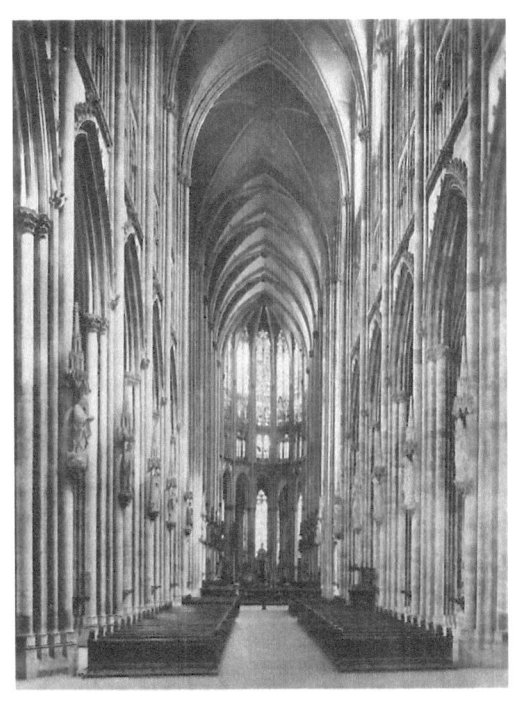

COLOGNE CATHEDRAL - INTERIOR

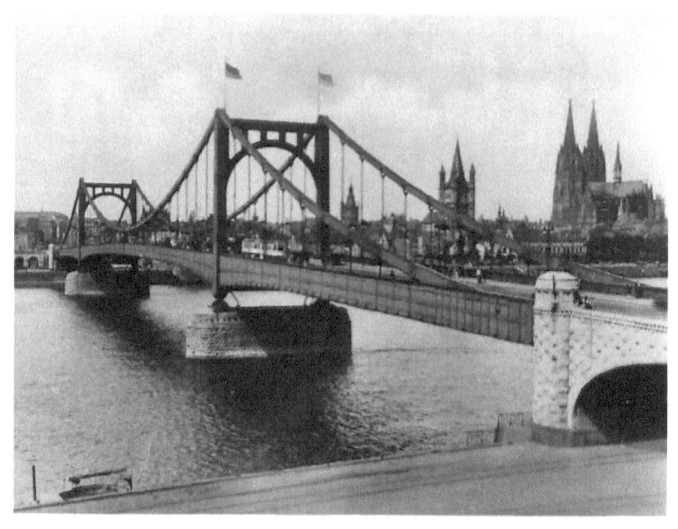

BRIDGE OVER THE RHINE - COLOGNE

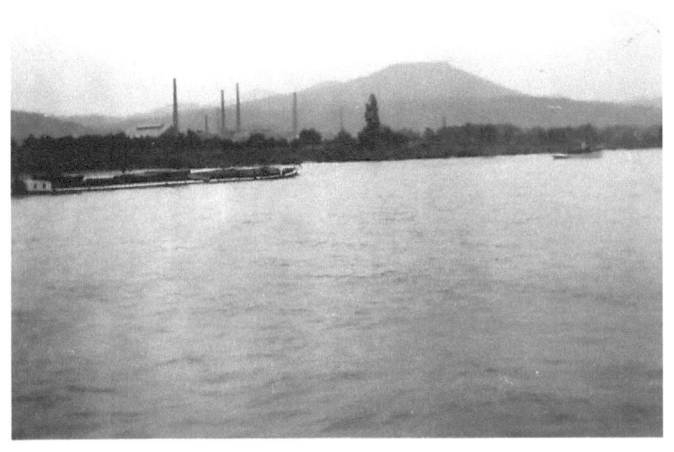

4 OF THE 7
MOUNTAINS ON THE
EAST BANK OF THE
RHINE

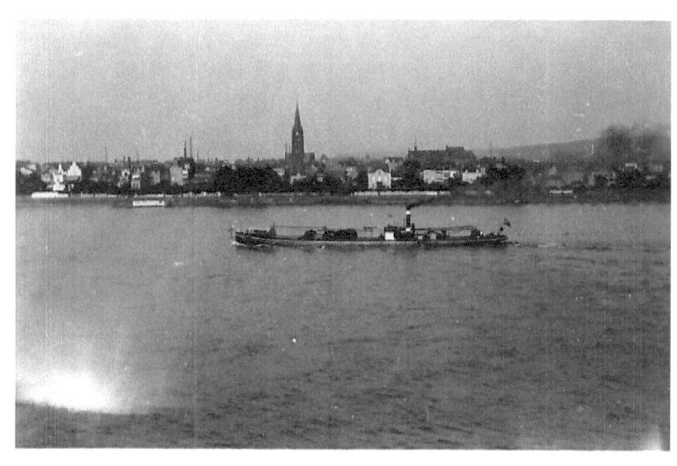

RIVER RHINE FROM BONN

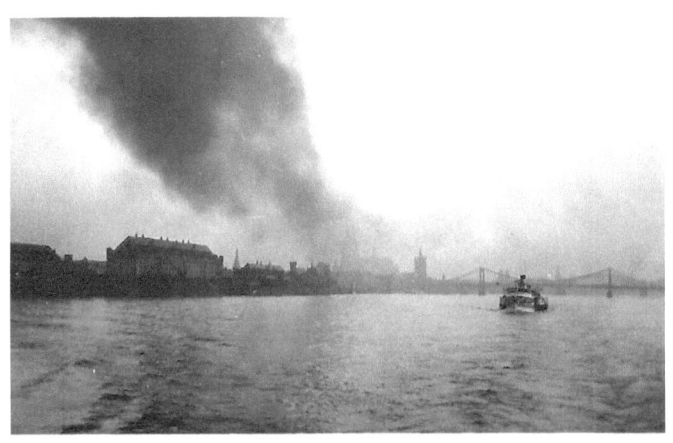

COLOGNE FROM
THE RHINE

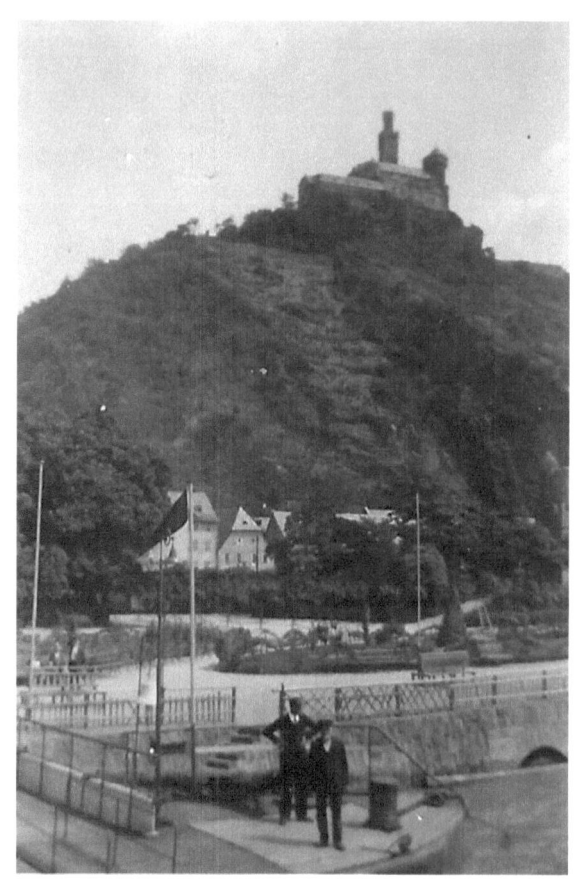

MARKSBURG CASTLE

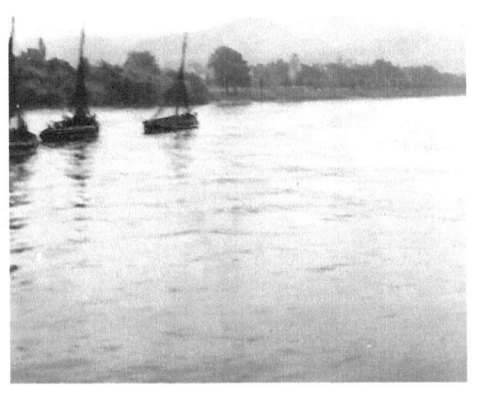

BOATS OF THE RHINE

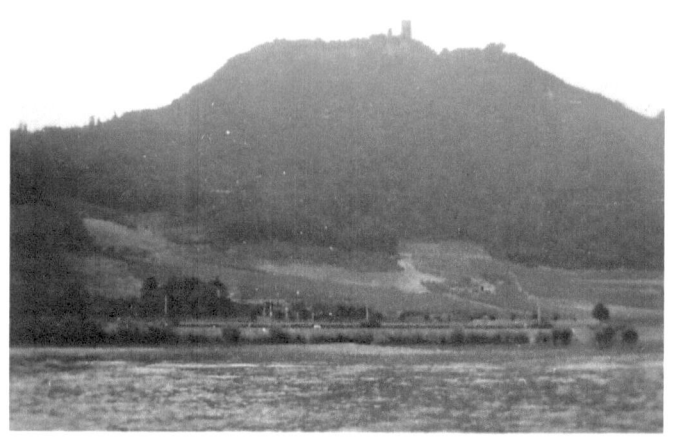

THE CASTLED CRAG
OF DRACHENFELS

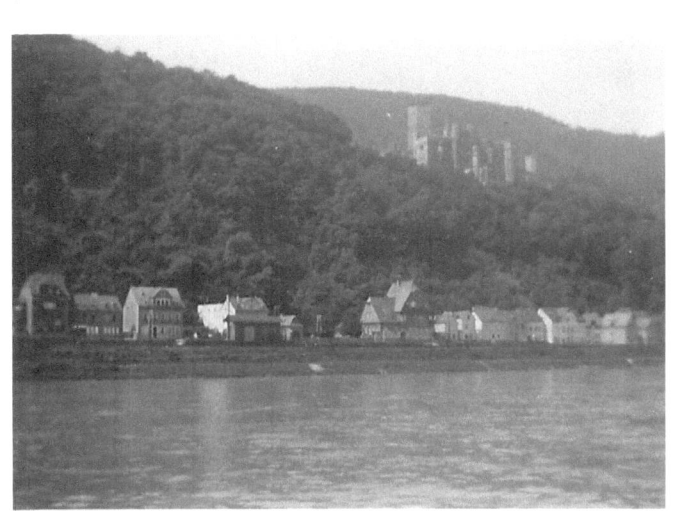

STOLZENFELS
CASTLE

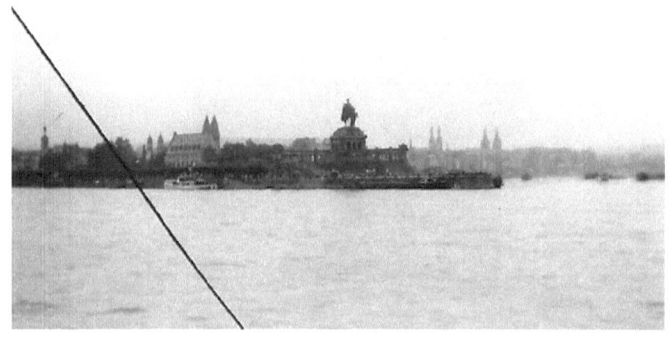

KOBLENZ FROM THE RHINE

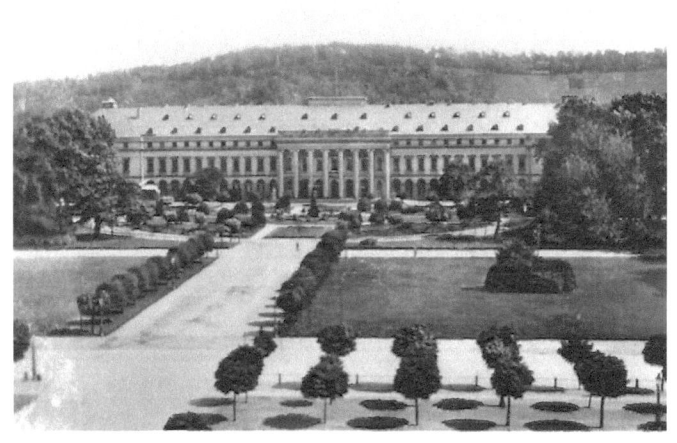

THE ELECTORAL
PALACE IN KOBLENZ

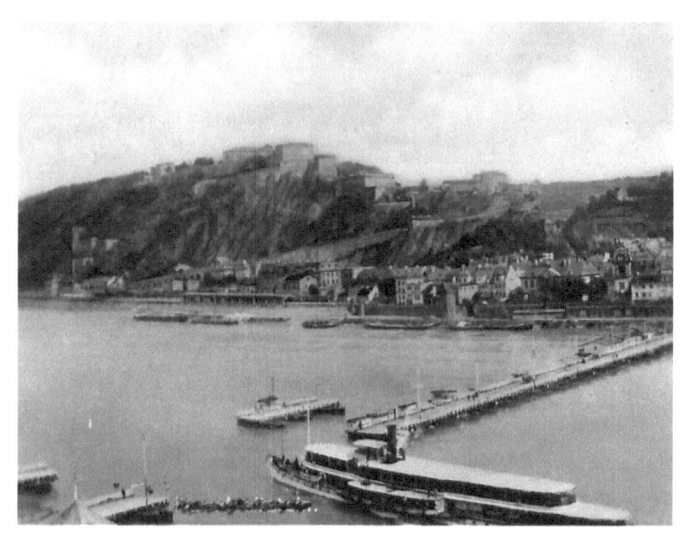

EHRENBREITSTEIN
FORTRESS

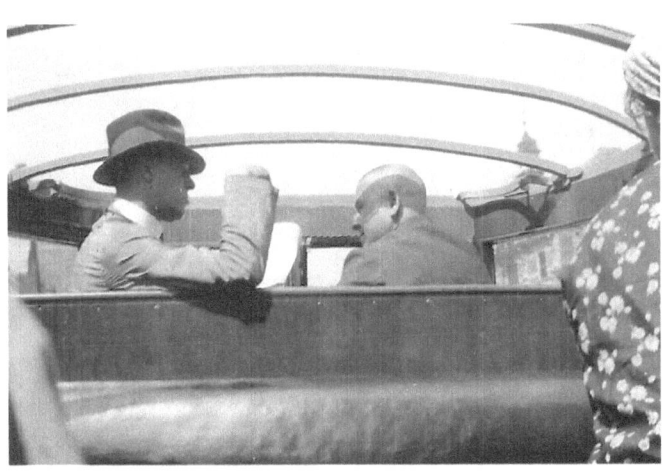

PASSENGERS ON
RIDE BESIDE RHINE

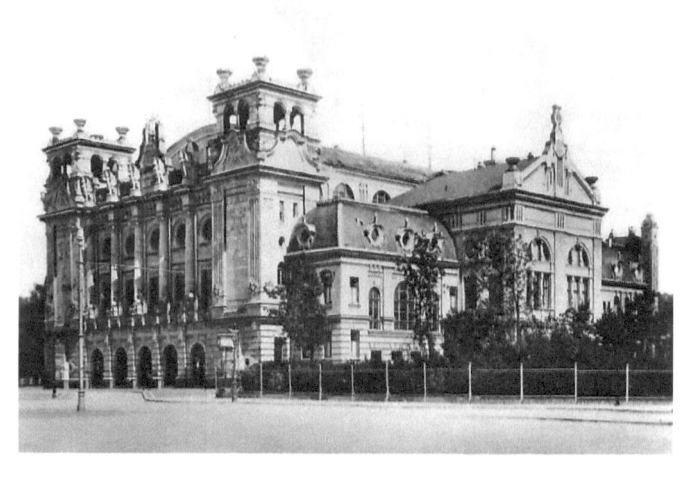

MUNICIPAL FESTIVAL HALL - KOBLENZ

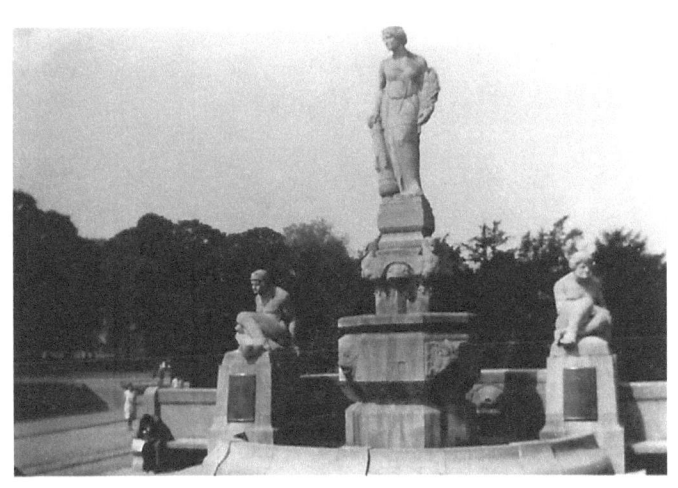

STATUE IN FRONT
OF THE MUNICIPAL
FESTIVAL HALL -
KOBLENZ

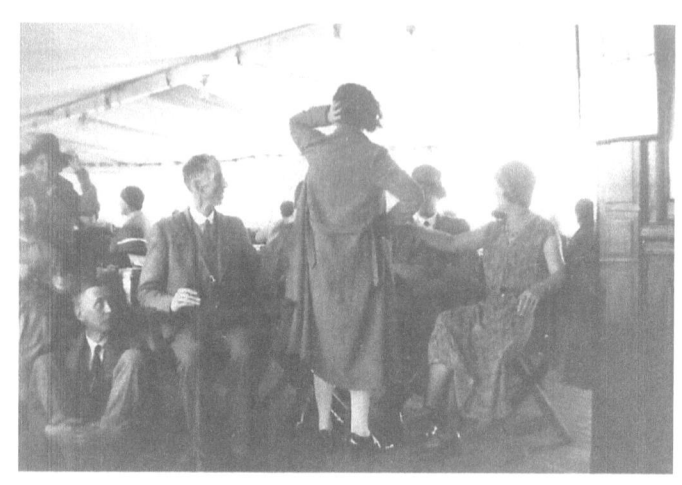

PEOPLE ON THE
RHINE

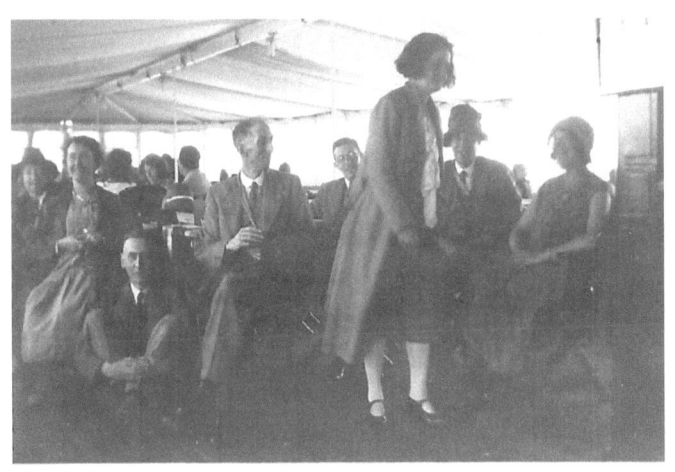

PEOPLE ON THE RHINE

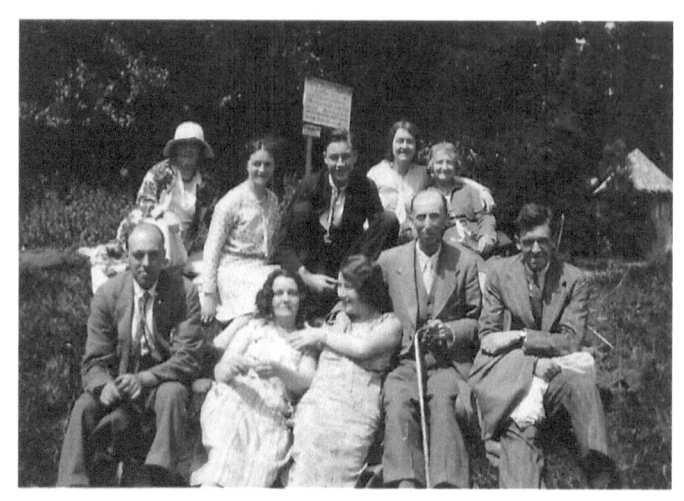

PEOPLE ON THE RIVER BANKS OF RHINE

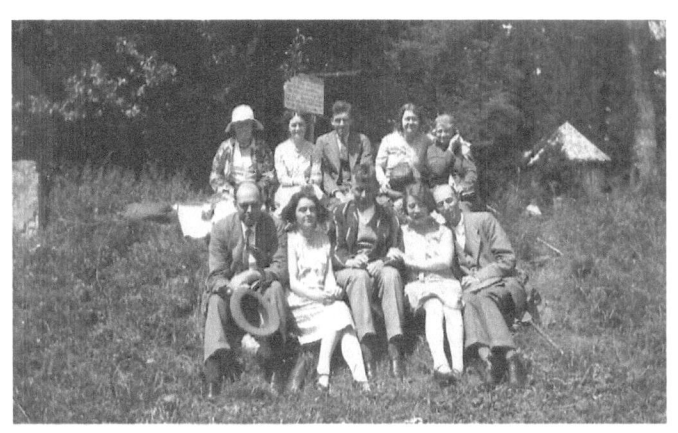

PEOPLE ON THE RIVER BANKS OF RHINE

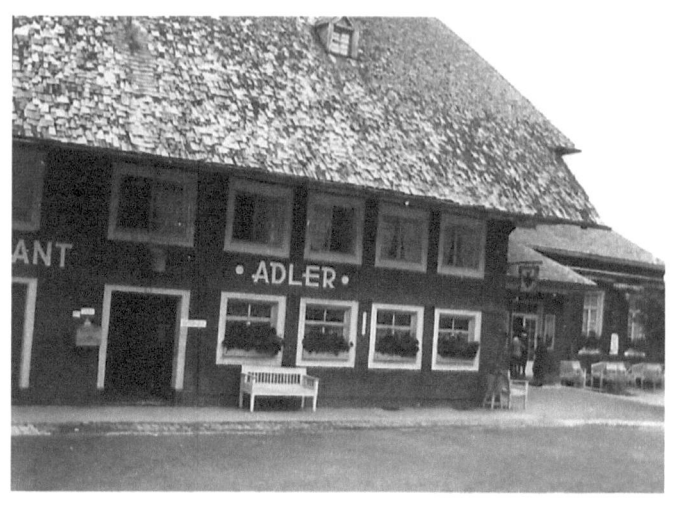

HOTEL ADLER -
HINTERZARTEN

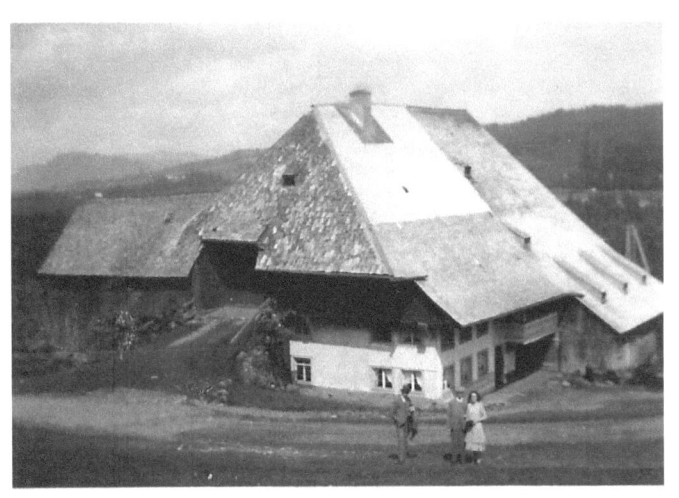

A BLACK FOREST
FARM HOUSE

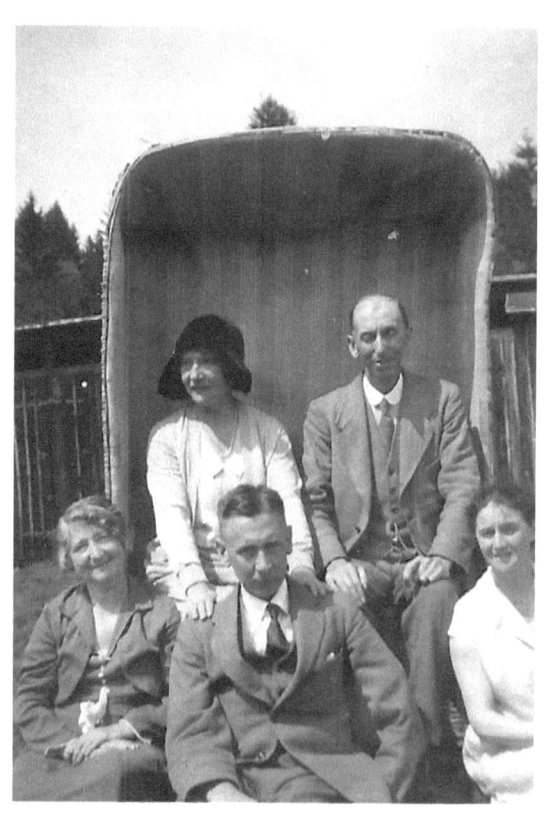

A BASKET
SUNBATHING CHAIR

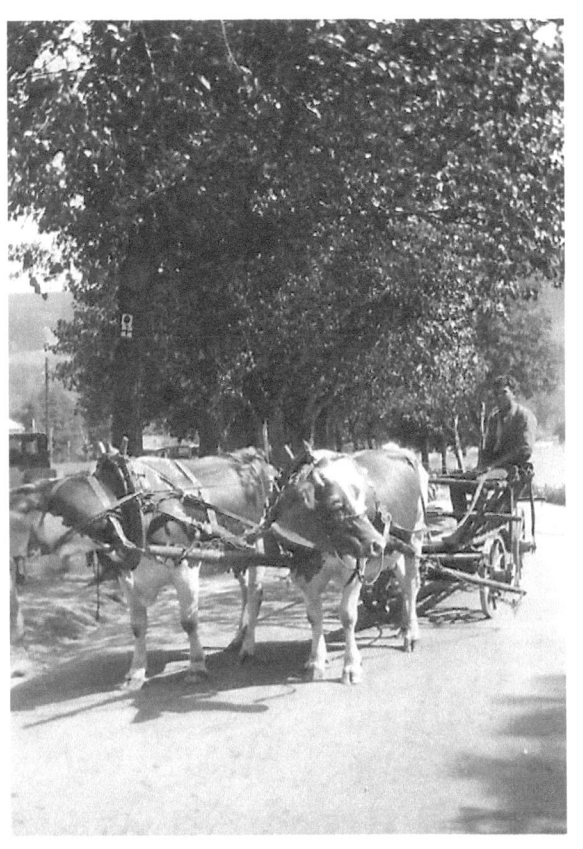

COW CART

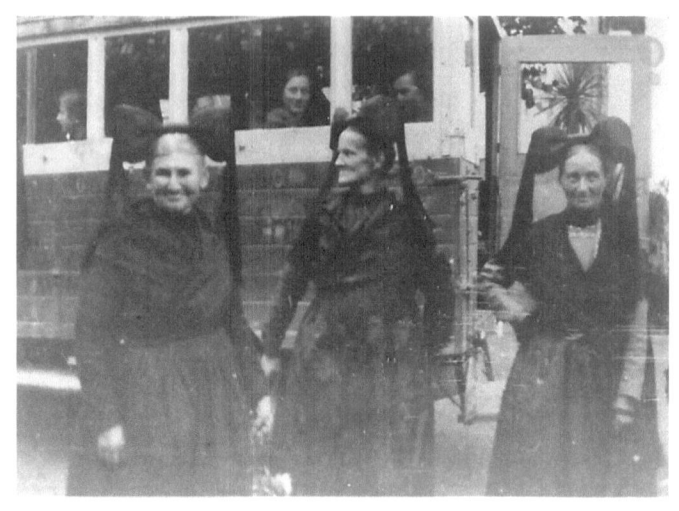

OLD WOMEN IN
THEIR SUNDAY
DRESSES ARRIVING
AT CHURCH IN A BUS

LAKE TITISEE

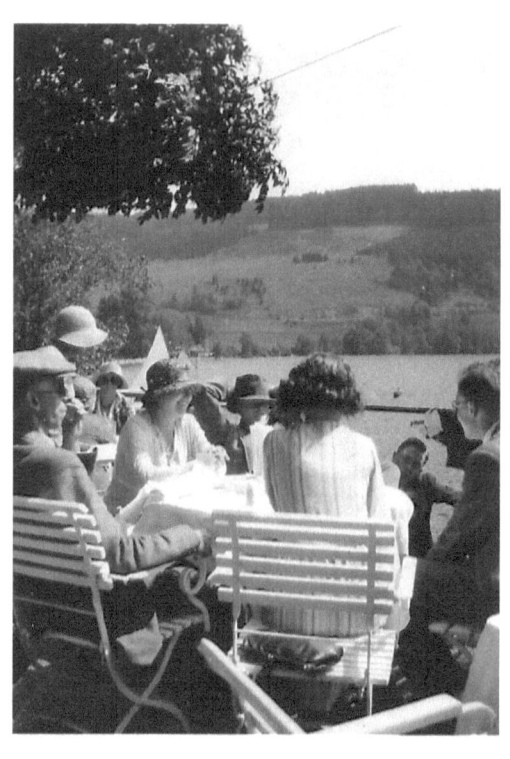

PEOPLE RESTING AT LAKE TITISEE

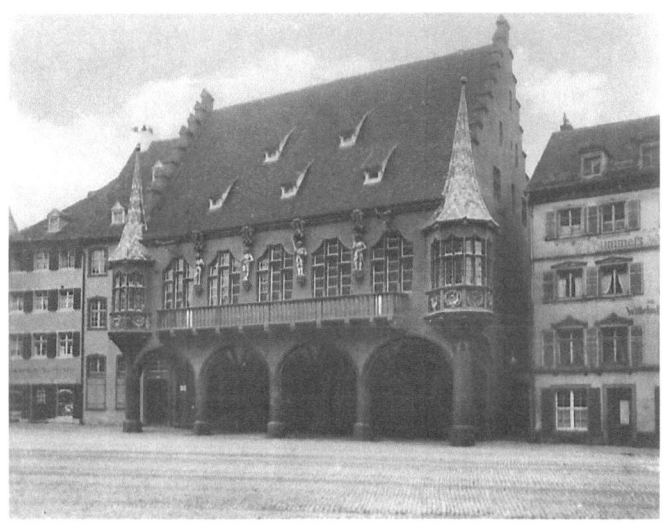

HISTORICAL
MERCHANTS' HALL
FREIBURG

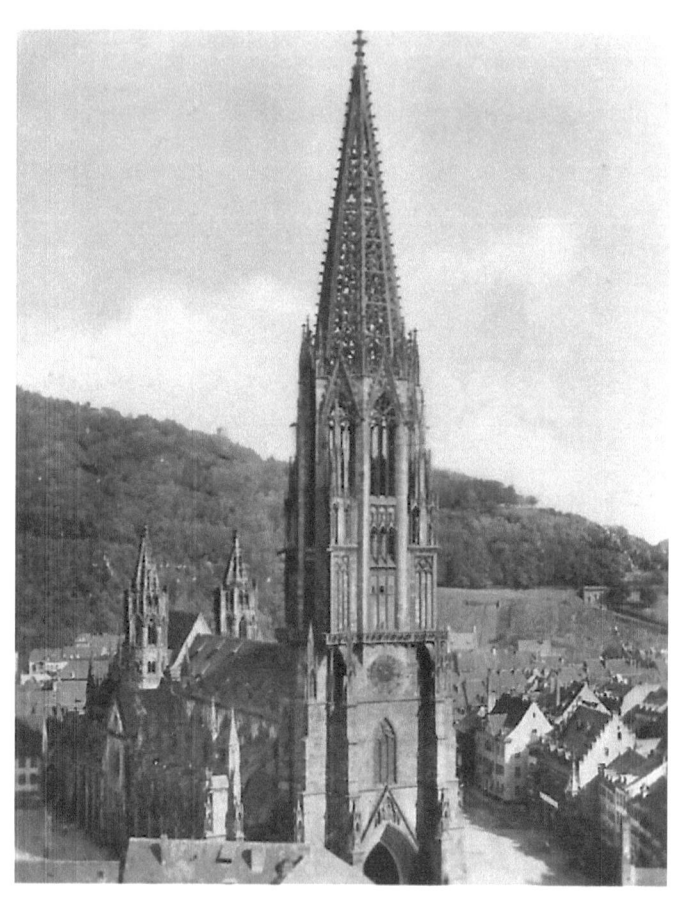

FREIBURG MINSTER

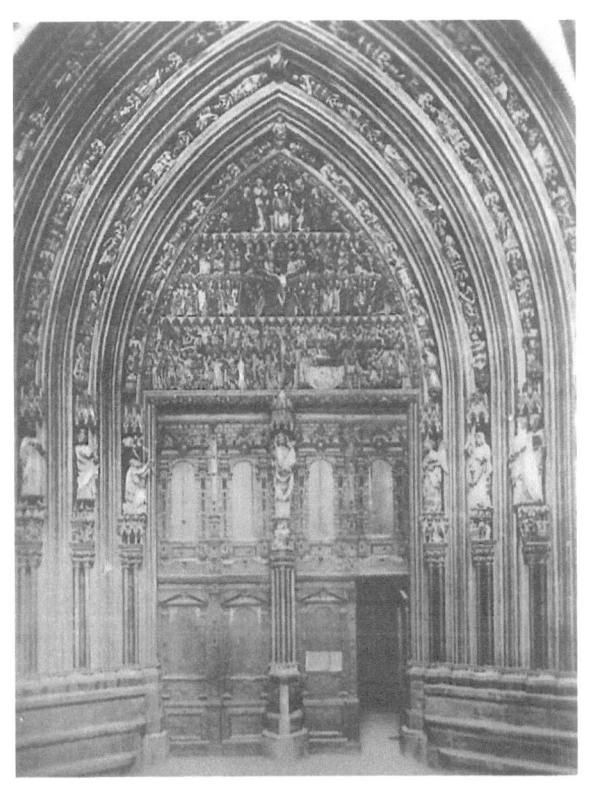

FREIBURG MINSTER
- WEST SIDE

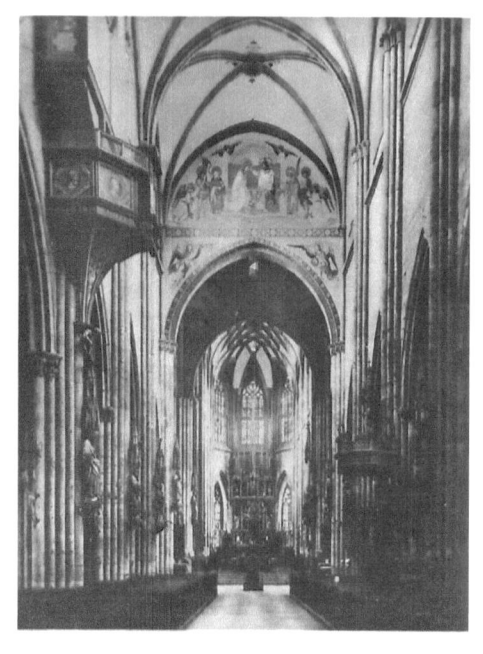

FREIBURG MINSTER
- INTERIOR

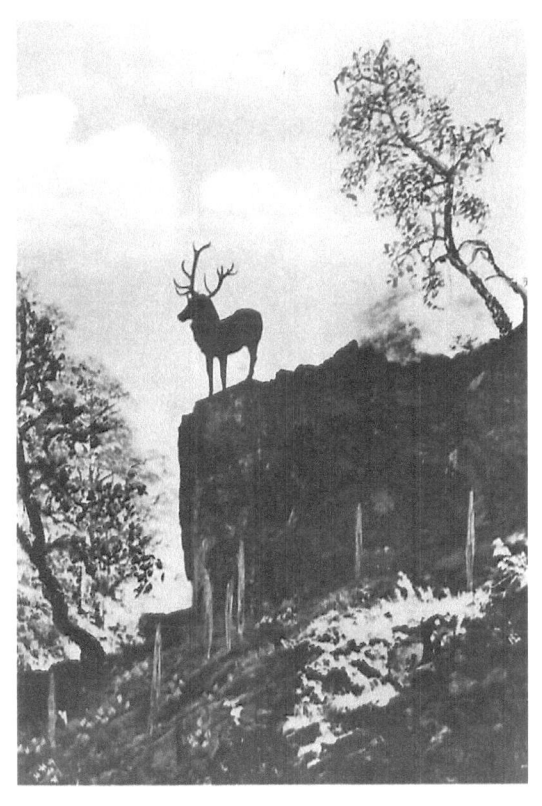

THE BLACK FOREST
- HIRSCHSPRUNG

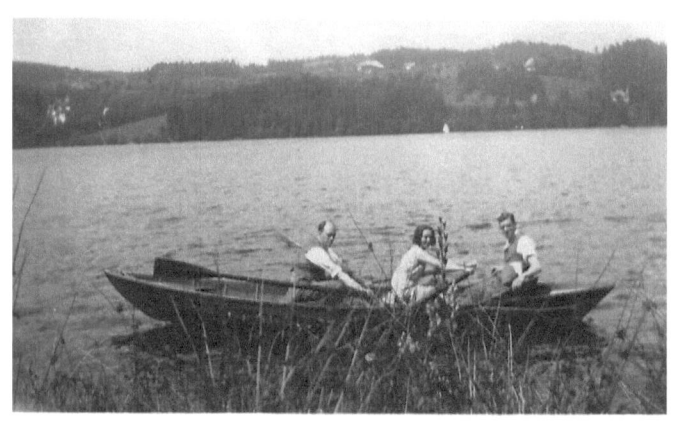

ROWING ON THE RHINE

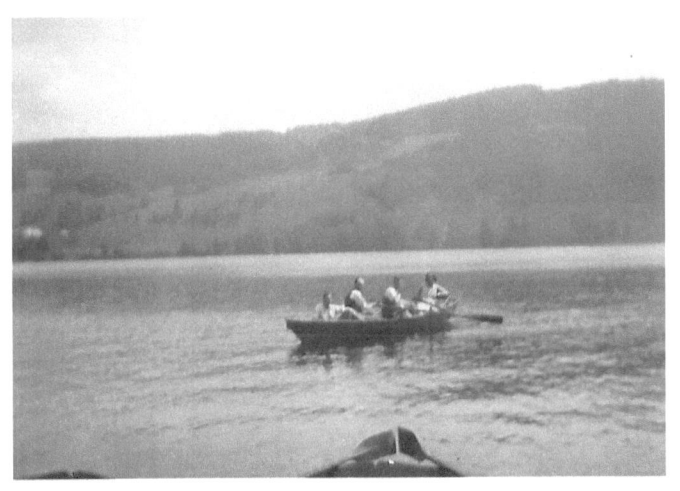

ROWING ON THE RHINE

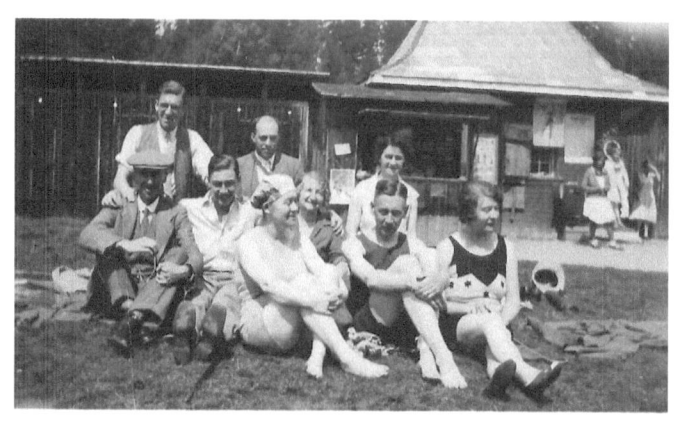

BATHING ON THE BANKS OF THE RHINE

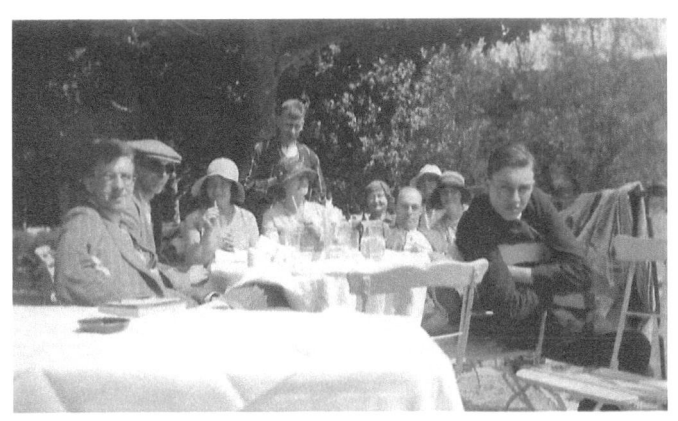

LUNCH ON THE BANKS OF THE RHINE

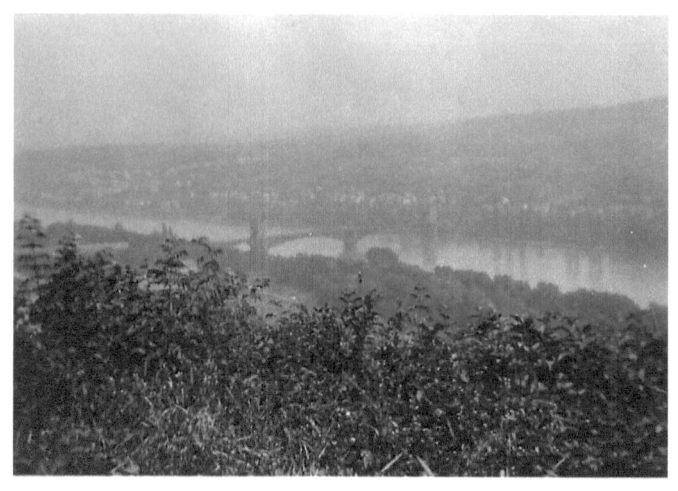

VIEW FROM
RITTERSTURZ

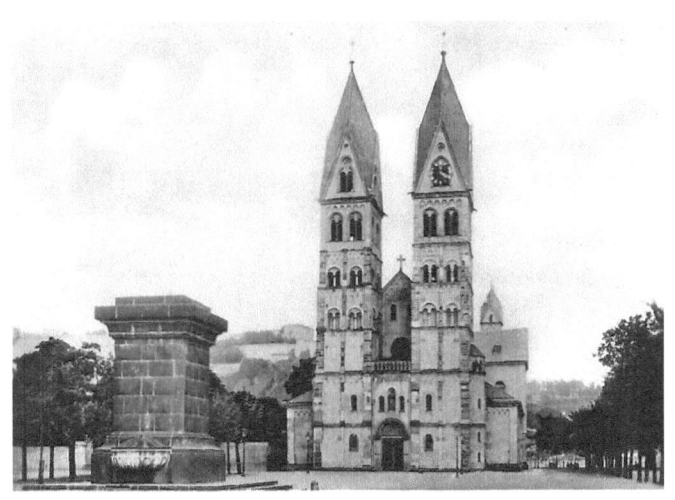

BASILICA OF ST. CASTOR

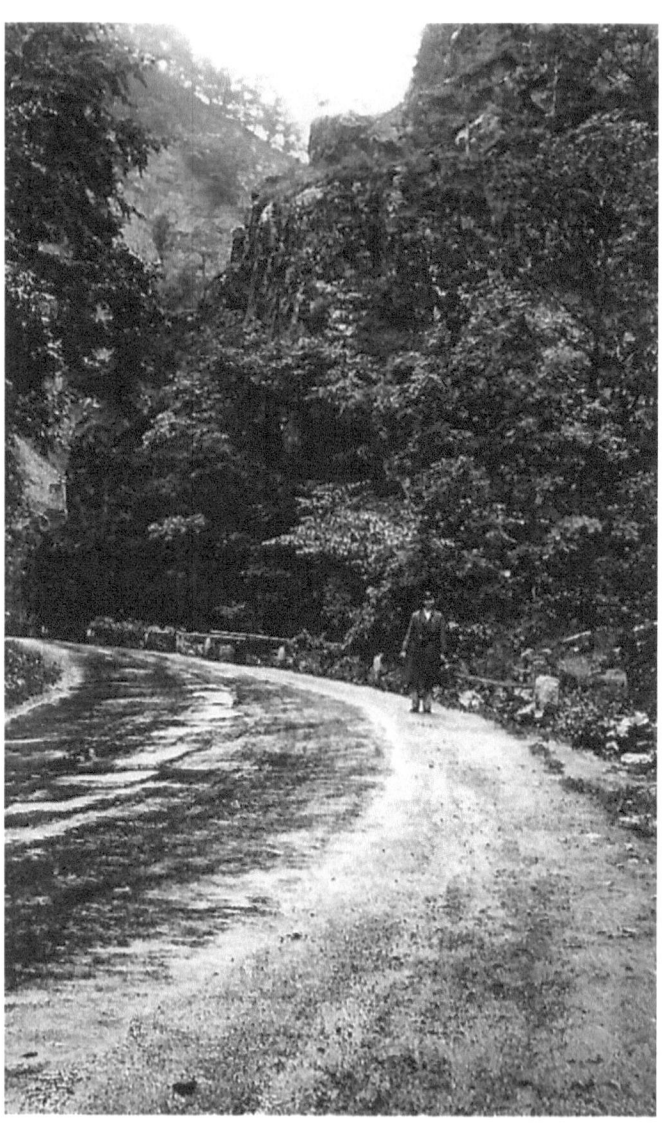

www.ingramcontent.com/pod-product-compliance
Lightning Source LLC
Chambersburg PA
CBHW020712180526

45163CB00008B/3048